Freud's Theories of the Unconscious and the
Psychological Analysis of Dreams

Pr Harry W. Chase

Freud's Theories of the Unconscious and the Psychological Analysis of Dreams

LM Publishers

Freud's Theories of the Unconscious

One upon a time it was the fashion to demonstrate witchcraft by sticking pins into the unlucky suspect. If any spots were found that appeared insensitive to pain, the unfortunate was forthwith declared a witch, with dire consequences to herself. Now-a-days such anesthesias are recognized, not as signs of a compact with the devil, but as symptoms of that mysterious disease of personality, hysteria.

This reversal of the point of view is typical. We have come to look upon many phenomena that were formerly ascribed to supernatural agencies – crystal gazing, second sight, hallucinations, double personality, possessions, ghosts, even mediumship – not as manifestations of supernatural powers, but as due to an abnormal condition of mind in the subject. In less enlightened days the Miss Beauchamp of whom Prince tells us in his "Dissociation of a Personality," who was several personalities by turns and had, as a rule, as one personality no recollection of the acts she performed as another, might have been burned as a witch. To-day she is a problem for the psychologist.

As knowledge of the psychological nature of such abnormal phenomena has grown, the need has increasingly been felt for some comprehensive explanation of their character. Here, for example, we have a girl (in a case reported by Janet) who has nursed her mother through a painful illness from consumption, resulting in death. The poverty of the family would not allow her even proper nourishment for her suffering mother. Her grief and despair may be imagined. But after the funeral she has apparently forgotten the whole series of events; the entire "complex" has dropped from consciousness. She is bewildered by any mention of the circumstances. But, on occasion, she falls into a trance-like state, in which she rehearses the circumstances of the illness and death of her mother with the utmost fidelity. And then, suddenly, she is normal again, but again she has no recollection of the crisis through which she has just passed. Here is a series of events apparently split off from her conscious personality altogether, yet instinct with energy that at time brings it to the surface. Here is another hysterical patient who has forgotten all about the shock that the physician suspects must have occurred as the starting point of her disease, and yet in hypnosis the whole thing comes out as vividly as ever. Consciously it could not be recalled, and yet it was existing and working; for it is a peculiarity of such split-off complexes that they may cause all sorts of conscious disturbances, though the patient him- self has forgotten all about the event which started the disturbances, or sees no connection between it and the disturbances which it has set up. Here, for instance, is a young German girl (the classic case of Anna 0. reported by Breuer and Freud), well educated, knowing some English, yet not using it as fluently as German. At a certain period in her life she suddenly becomes unable to speak or read her mother- tongue, and is obliged to use English altogether. Finally, in a hypnoidal state, she remembers that, once while she was watching by the bedside of her father, she was frightened by a sudden hallucination. Terrified, she tried to pray, but all that came into her mind were the words of an old English nursery rhyme. The shock, and her manner of reaction to it, caused her to forget her German, and to retain only the English, which had come to her aid at this critical period. There was no connection in her mind between the shock and the disturbances which it had left behind, yet the association, though not a conscious one, had been set up somewhere, somehow.

But all this is abnormal. We do not have to go so far afield to see instances of the same mysterious workings. Who of us has not had the experience of giving up a knotty point in despair for the time, to come back to it and find that our ideas had somehow fallen into place, had apparently worked themselves over without our help. Or how often a name that we have tried unsuccessfully to recall pops into our mind in the midst of some other train of thought. In such cases we have not been dealing with conscious activities as we know them. What has been the process ? What has been going on ?

It is such considerations as these that have led to the building up of theories of unconscious action, which fill out the gaps in our conscious life. By unconscious action we understand action which goes on without our being aware of it, and yet which seems intelligent, adapted to a purpose. In short, it is activity which it is hard to differentiate from conscious action, except in its lack of this very property of awareness. Most psychologists to-day admit that activities which are more or less like conscious activities go on under the threshold of consciousness; but the orthodox psychological explanation is that they are mere physiological activities, complex changes in the neurons, and that there is nothing mental about them. The brain itself is so complex, they say, that there is no need of supposing that we really think and feel unconsciously, all that occurs is a change in physiological arrangement. The mental and the conscious are co-extensive terms. On the other hand, those who have dealt most with the abnormal phenomena, and are less at home in the field of pure psychology, see in such conscious activities something mental as well. The phenomena are so complex, they say, that if they occurred in an animal, for example, we would unhesitatingly call them mental. They are of course physiological, hut it is hard to explain their apparent intelligence without sup- posing that they are mental as well. The conflict is very like that now waging between the two schools of animal psychologists, those who would reduce everything in the life of the animal to a series of mechanical reflexes, and those who look for signs of conscious intelligence. Like this conflict, too, it is one which can never be decided by introspection, it is only as results accumulate that the balance will swing to one side or the other. In accordance with the law of economy that regulates scientific thinking, it would seem that such activities ought to be explained in physiological terms if it is possible to do so ; in this ease the question becomes: are they too complex to be so explained?

The thing of all others most needful here, then, would seem to be more evidence as to the nature of such unconscious activities. Such a body of evidence has been brought forward by Professor Freud, of Vienna, whose work is just beginning to be known in this country. Professor Freud is primarily an alienist, a former student of Charcot at the Salpetriere. In the course of a long practise with neurotic patients, he has arrived gradually at theories of the mechanism of the unconscious, which, if they are substantiated, will go far to revolutionize present psychological conceptions.

Freud's theory is unique in that he supposes the region of the unconscious to be built up of two distinct layers, and that he would explain all the facts of unconscious action as due to the interaction of these two layers.

The upper layer is a sort of vestibule to consciousness. When, for example, as in the case cited above, we try in vain to recall a name, and later find it coming of itself into consciousness, Freud would explain the case as follows : The train of conscious activity set up by the effort has, as soon as attention was turned away from it, sunk below the threshold of consciousness. But it does not at once die away. The activity rather goes on exactly as though it were in consciousness, new associative connections are made, and by and by the associative train succeeds in reaching the name of which we were in search. This now appears in consciousness, seemingly out of all associative connection, and yet a train of association has led to its discovery, only it was a train of unconscious association. So during the day we break off scores of trains of thought without carrying them to a conclusion, because they are too trivial, too complex, too unwelcome, to occupy the mind further. Such trains of thought drop below the threshold, and there may form new associative connections. If these are strong enough, they may again appear above the threshold, apparently without cause. If such connections are not formed readily, the activity may die out without effect. Or such a train of thought may form still other associations, and sink to lower depths of the soul, still to be considered. This upper layer of the unconscious, then, which we find in Freud's theory, is very like the usual sense in which the word "unconscious" is used, especially by those who would see something mental in its activities.

But the unique contribution which Freud has made to the subject is in his theory of the lower layer of the unconscious, which is in many respects totally different in its structure and activities from the upper layer which we have been considering. In order to see his conception more clearly, let us follow for a moment the development of the individual. We all know that the child exhibits many tendencies which in the adult would be signs of criminality, insanity or abnormality. Our conscious personality as it exists today is the result of a long process of growth, each stage built on the ruins of the one beneath. The child is savage, primitive ; it is only by degrees that he becomes adapted to the restraints of our modern civilization, and represses his old activities. But now, says Freud, such repressed activities leave their traces behind. They may not seem to affect us consciously ; we may have even forgotten many of the old ways of thinking and acting, but their traces still exist. What has become of the energy which went to the gratification of our old selfish, individual, feral, modes of thought and action ? With most of us the energy has found for the most part new outlets, it has produced the motive force for new developments. It has been " sublimated " to higher uses. But the draining off of the energy from the old modes of action has not been complete. The old primitive tendencies still persist unconsciously in the best of us, and will crop out in some form or other if the provocation be sufficient. We have repressed our childish desires so long that we may have forgotten that they ever existed, but yet they are not quite dead. Particularly is this true in the realm of sex — for Freud holds that the child has a sex life of his own as truly as the adult. It has, to be sure, not yet come to a head in the sexual organs, but it is none the less existent, and in ways which in the adult would be called perversions; which, indeed, if not repressed, are the origin of perversions in later life. Now these old ways of sexual satisfaction are usually repressed under the influence of the environment, yet the tendency to their gratification still exists; we may see it cropping out in the most normal of us in dreams, for example. The energy that went to the satisfaction of such impulses has for the most part been drained off into new channels, but a little of it still remains locked up with the old complexes. Perhaps none of us have as much energy at our disposal for mental work as we ought to have, for some of it still is attached to old and outworn tendencies, making it a little easier and a little more possible for them to come into operation under favoring circumstances than for new tendencies so to do.

Now, for Freud, it is of just such cast off complexes, each with its own complement of energy, that the lowest level of the unconscious is made up. All the unethical acts and unsocial ways of thought of the child, repugnant to us to-day, still exist in the lowest dark chamber of the soul, not strong enough to break out into action, but alive. It is the penalty which we pay for our civilization, that it imposes standards of thought and action which are foreign to the deepest tendencies in us, modes of life of the cave-man and the ages before civilization, which have left their marks on the soul forever. And for all of us there has been some strain in adjusting to its requirements, resulting in the abandonment after a struggle of the old racial ways, and the substitution of newer and more ethical modes of action. But a part of our personality still remains in the troglodytic stage. We may not allow this part expression ; we may not even be conscious that it longer exists, and yet it lives and works below the threshold, just as the remembrance of the death of her mother still affected the girl, though consciously it had lapsed. With the split between childhood and adolescence, the chasm between the old and the new becomes still wider; we turn our back more and more on the old ways; they lapse from consciousness more and more completely. Childhood seems a little alien to all of us; there has been a "transvaluation of all values' so that the remembrance of how we thought and felt then comes to us with the mark of a little strangeness upon it. It is strange just because we have cast it all out, we have "put away childish things." But in the dark limbo of the unconscious they still live on, unconscious though we may be that such is the case. The lowest level of the unconscious is thus far removed from consciousness in its modes of functioning. The conception that such tendencies still function, still need continual, though not conscious repression, is the essential point here.

But now what is the mechanism that prevents us from knowing that these old tendencies are still striving upward toward conscious expression? Consciousness is guarded from a knowledge of their existence and their activities, holds Freud, by the interposition of the upper level of the unconscious. This acts like a censor, a guard at the gate, and will not admit to conscious expression these outworn complexes, because of the pain which they would cause us if we were compelled to take account of them in our thinking. It would require too much energy consciously to keep them down ; so it is the function of the upper level of the unconscious to save consciousness all this trouble, and to leave it free for other things. This it does, in ordinary circumstances, so well that we are not even aware that any repression is going on, or, indeed, that there is anything to repress. We have repressed our old complexes so long and so well that the act of repression has dropped below the conscious level; we are not aware of its existence. But, on the other hand, it is continually going on, for the old complexes are always striving up to expression. And so the system of energy in the unconscious is a two-way system; the upper system keeping down the lower. If this be true, how different is our mind from the report which consciousness gives us. Outwardly, all is calm and placid, and yet beneath the surface is the mighty conflict always going on. We are like citizens sleeping in security while outside the gates the battle rages hot between our protectors and our enemies. Fortunately, it is our protectors who are usually victorious ; the repressive force of the upper level is strong enough to prevent the emergence of the denizens of the lower stages. But this is not always so. Occasionally the assailants find a breach in the fortifications, or a weak spot in the line of battle, and echoes of the conflict come to us within.

To abandon figures, the lower level of the unconscious may under certain circumstances win a partial victory, and some feature of the old complex may arise in our minds. This may happen in the following way. Suppose that a train of thought broken off during the day, and sinking to the upper level of the unconscious, works out there to a conclusion which permits it to be brought into associative connection with one of the complexes on the lower level. The whole process has been unconscious; we are not aware that such a connection has been made, and yet in the trivial event of the day there has been some element, some common feeling tone, some phrase, some suggestion, which is like enough to the old complex to form an associative connection with it. Suppose that during the day we express some slight concern about the health of a near relative, and, in the pressure of work, forget about the matter. Under the threshold, on the upper level, this train of thought may spread further. Now it is one of the traits of children that they have at first little sympathy and love for their younger brothers and sisters. It is not uncommon for them to express a wish that they would die, that they might have more attention from their parents. For death for the child means of course only an absence ; he has no conception of its real significance. But such an idea is foreign to the adult mind ; it has been so repressed and was expressed at so early a stage that we can hardly realize that it ever existed. However, on Freud's theory, it still does exist, and is continually being repressed by the upper levels. Suppose now that the train of thought having to do with the health of the relative in question works out to a conclusion below the threshold which tends to call up the old complex. This is at once given new energy, its repression is more difficult. And yet it does not emerge consciously. But at night, when the inhibitions are down in sleep, when the repressive force is not quite so great, it makes a supreme effort, and gets through — in a dream. We may awaken terrified from a dream of the death of the same relative who caused us the concern during the day; what gave the motive force to the dream was the old childhood complex, which in this case has, by the help of the new energy, succeeded in breaking through into consciousness. For Freud, the motive force behind a dream is always that of some old complex in the depths of the soul ; the dream is a deeply significant revelation of the true nature of our unconscious life, to him who knows how to read it.

This last qualification is important, for it usually happens that the inhibiting force, though not able to completely prevent the emergence of the buried complex, distorts it almost beyond recognition, so that the dream seems to us absurd, disconnected, void of all meaning. This distortion is sometimes so complete that there is only here and there a hint of the true meaning of the dream; it seems to be made up from trivial events of the day alone ; but in such cases close examination will show that rational association of such events has been carried on through the complex, which has served as the connecting link and given new energy which permits the trivial events to recur in the dream, though openly the complex does not appear at all. Such was the dream of the woman who saw her nephew lying dead, and yet felt no grief. Now it chanced that on the day before, she had bought a ticket to see her lover, from whom she had parted, in a public performance, and was looking forward eagerly to the event. Some of the details of the dream seemed to suggest that there was some association with this fact; and, indeed, it was found on analysis that the last time she had seen her lover was at the funeral of another nephew. It was as though she had said to herself, "If my other nephew dies, I shall see him again.' Do we not perhaps see here the activity of the old childish way of thinking that would sacrifice anything for a moment's happiness for the individual ? And yet that complex had not appeared at all in the dream as such. It is thus

Freud's thesis that the dream never says what it means, that it is the product of a compromise between the two systems of energy. The complex is distorted in getting around the censor, and thus there arise all sorts of symbolic and indirect ways of expression; the complex is only alluded to in the dream in allegorical ways, or under cover of the trivial events of the day that stand in connection with it ; it is not expressed directly. Blood and fire in dreams may appear as sexual symbols ; the symbolism may be very complex, as in the case of some of the symbols of primitive man ; associations may be determined in the most superficial ways; for example, one person may stand for another in a dream on no more basis of identification than that both wear eyeglasses. The complex makes use of any possible associative connections in order to utilize a little energy to strengthen itself. And it is of course also true that the more indirect and symbolic the associations, the less likely we are to suspect the complexes which are manifesting themselves through them, and so much the more likely will the complex be to avoid the censor. It is as though the complex, in its mad desire to escape, disguised itself and slipped around the back way. It succeeds in escaping, but its disguise alters it so beyond recognition that even its best friends will not recognize it.

Thus in the dream we see the conflict of the two systems of energy, and, if we are skilled, we may even interpret the signs as the woodsman would do, and tell what complex has passed that way, and how it was clad. For the first time the psychology of dreams is thus given a coherent setting, which shows it as a type of activity not foreign to our usual modes of thought, but of one piece with them. For the dream is only one illustration of this conflict.

What, says Freud, are the symbols of the artist and the poet but just such disguises, the product of the conflict in his own soul between the primitive and the civilized ways of thought ? Other observers have already shown that the root of art is in sex ; here we see that it is through the symbolism of a sex-conflict that it develops.

Now, suppose that the complexes are a little stronger, have not been as well suppressed as in the normal individual ; in such a case they may break out as hysterical symptoms or obsessions — yet the emergence is not complete, though more complete than in the dream, for the individual still has gaps in his conscious memory with regard to the ways in which the complexes are connected with his symptoms, or he may have forgotten the origin of some of his symptoms altogether. And yet in every case his neurosis goes back and roots in the strength of just such complexes, which have seized on events of his adult life somewhat similar to them in nature, and through the breaches thus made have burst forth into a real, if detached, life.

Shocks, traumatic experiences, cause forgetfulness and splitting of personality, on this theory, because they resemble sufiiciently in some respect the old childhood complexes, and these latter are for one reason or another so strong that the experience forms its associative connections with the older complexes, and not with conscious personality. So it drops below the level of consciousness, to in turn strive to rise to the surface. The hysterical symptom is then a symbol of the conflict between the two tendencies. If there were no conflict the old complex would emerge wholly; that it emerges in indirect and symbolic ways is additional proof of the conflict which is going on. One must, then, have reached a certain stage of ethical development, must have repressed old tendencies, in order to develop a neurosis.

It is of course true that this repression of the lower by the upper is in general good for the organism; it is well that consciousness should be left free. The fact that it miscarries at times and a neurosis or a nightmare ensues is only because of the relative strength of the complexes, and not because of a defect inherent in the system itself.

Thus for Freud the most real part of the drama of the soul goes on behind the scenes. Most things that we think we do from conscious motives, most of the thoughts that come into our minds, are but the surrogates and the symbols for the processes that go on beneath the threshold. Ideas are so censored before they get admission to consciousness that we have often little notion of their real nature, and can only wonder that the apparently meaningless idea should haimt us so.

If these conclusions are substantiated, we seem to have a new light shed on the old question of the unconscious. It becomes for us the most real part of ourselves; the expression of our deepest tendencies. It is a realm far larger and far deeper than consciousness; it holds secrets that we thought lost forever. The psychologist would explain the unconscious from the nature of consciousness; Freud, on the other hand, explains consciousness from the nature and function of the unconscious.

The assertion that much of our thinking is symbolic in its nature, due to the fact that it serves as a sort of safety-valve for the escape of our repressed complexes, is of course a problem which can never be solved by appeal to consciousness alone. And it is so with most of the other positions which Freud has taken; we are following pathways where introspection is no guide. Thus he would have us shift the emphasis in psychology from a study of consciousness over to a study of the unconscious. Consciousness, for him, is but the surface; it is in the depths below consciousnes that true reality is found.

We may then sum up the contribution which Freud has made to the psychology of the unconscious as follows: he has supposed that the unconscious consists of two streams of tendencies, or energy, one stream striving to revive all the time experiences which would be repugnant to us, and which we have outgrown, and the other striving to check the revival of such tendencies. As a result of this conflict, we have introduced into our thoughts and acts, especially in conditions when barriers are somewhat down (as in dreams, lapses, neuroses, reveries), a vast deal of the symbolic and the indirect methods of presentation.

Now is such activity as we have been considering mental in its nature — are the unconscious associations and connections of which we have been speaking really associations and thoughts that go on underneath the surface? Or are we dealing with a very complex degree of nervous activity, and with that alone? Freud nowhere states his own position definitely, though it is perhaps too easy to accuse him of leanings toward the mental interpretation. What he has done is rather to open up new lines of approach to the problem, to give us a consistent and closely reasoned interpretation of observed facts. Psychologists are beginning to recognize that, right or wrong, he must be reckoned with. He has given a stimulus to work along this line that may go a long way toward the ultimate solution of some of our baffling psycho- logical problems.

The Psychological Analysis of Dreams[1]

It is not an uncommon phenomenon in the development of science that professional men of erudition, with all the help at their disposal, with all the implements of their knowledge and ability, combat some principle of popular wisdom which is, on the other hand, defended by the people with equal tenacity, and that finally science is forced to recognize that in essentials the popular conception, and not its own, is correct. It would be especially worthy of investigation to discover why it is that science, on its gradually mounting path, progresses in an irregular zigzag line, which at times comes close to the popular *Weltanschauung*, and then quite departs from it.

---

[1] by Sándor Ferenczi, translated by Pr Harry W. Chase

I mention this peculiar phenomenon for the reason that the latest investigations of dreams, those noteworthy and bizarre manifestations of mental life, have laid bare facts which compel us to abandon our former views of the nature of dreams, and, with certain limitations, to return to the popular theory.

The people have never given up a belief in the significance of dreams. The oldest writings which have been preserved to us, hewn out in stone in praise of the old Babylonian kings, as also the mythology and history of the Hindoos, Chinese, Aztecs, Greeks, Etruscans, Jews and Christians, take the point of view, held to-day by the mass of the people, that dreams can be interpreted. The interpretation of dreams was for thousands of years a special science, a particular cult, whose priests and priestesses often decided the fate of countries and called forth revolutions which changed the history of the world. This now antiquated science rested on the unshakable belief that the dream, though in a concealed way and by obscure analogies, was quite capable of interpretation by the initiate, revealed the future, and that by these nocturnal phenomena the higher powers desired to prepare mortals for approaching events of importance. In the lower ranks of the populace, the dream book, that noteworthy survival of ancient Babylonian astrology, still enjoys to-day great popularity and is much used. Although the details of the dream-books differ in essentials from each other in the different countries, they must be considered products of the common folk-spirit.

On the other hand, we find on the part of the great majority of recent psychologists an almost complete contempt for the dream as a psychic function, and as a result a denial also that the dream-content is of any significance. Many of these investigations consider the dream to be a senseless complex of hallucinations, which blaze up in a lawless way in the brain of the sleeper. According to the view of others, the dream is nothing but the psychic reaction to these outer (objective) or inner (subjective) stimuli, which the sensory end-organs of the body receive during sleep and conduct to the centres.

There were only a few who held the theory that the sleeping psyche could develop a complicated, significant activity, or that the dream could be maintained to have any sort of a symbolic meaning. But even these latter did not succeed in making the peculiarities of dreams comprehensible, without forcing their explanations into the Procrustian bed of an artificial playing with allegories.

Accordingly for centuries the army of superstitious interpreters of dreams stood over against that of the sceptics, until about ten years ago the Viennese neurologist, Professor Freud, discovered facts which make possible a unification of the two hostile conceptions, and which aided on the one hand in the discovery of the true nucleus in the age-old superstition, and on the other hand fully satisfied the scientific need of the knowledge of the connections between cause and effect.

I may say at this point, that Freud's theory of dreams and his method of interpretation only approach the popular conception in so far as to ascribe to dreams sense and meaning. But the newly discovered facts sustain in no way the belief of those who would base dreams on the interference of higher powers, and see prophecies in them. Freud's theory considers the dream as a mental product dependent upon endopsychic occurrences, and is not calculated to strengthen the belief of those who consider the dream as a device of higher powers or as the clairvoyance of the sleeper.

Psychoanalysis, a new method of investigation and treatment of psychoneuroses, made it possible for Freud to recognize the true significance of dreams. The method has its point of departure in the principle that the symptoms of these diseases are only the sensory images of particular thought-constellations, impregnated with feeling, which were distasteful to consciousness and therefore repressed, forgotten, but still live on in the unconscious; and in the fact that the surrogate-creations for the repressed material vanish as soon as the unconscious thought can be brought to light and made conscious by help of free association. In the course of this analytic work the dreams of the patients were told, and Freud made their content also an object of psychoanalytic investigation. To his surprise he found in dream analysis not only a great aid to the treatment of neuroses, but he gained at the same time as a byproduct a new explanation of the dream as a psychic function, more enlightening than any of the former explanations. In many chemical processes materials are incidentally obtained by the reduction of certain chemicals, which perhaps have been thrown away as useless for a long time, but which are shown after a time to be valuable materials, often surpassing the principal products of the manufacture in value. The case was about the same with the explanation of dreams incidentally found by Freud; it opens up such outlooks for the knowledge of both the sound and the diseased mind that in comparison its particular point of departure, the treatment of certain phenomena of nervous diseases, seems a scientific question of the second rank.

In the short time at my disposal I cannot reproduce exhaustively Freud's theory of dreams. I must rather confine myself to the more essential explanations and the most valuable facts of the new theory, and to its verification by examples. I do not imagine that this lecture will convince my hearers. According to my previous experience one can gain a conviction in affairs of psychoanalysis only for himself. So I shall not controvert here the lesser and quite superficial critics of Freud, but will rather explain in brief the most essential parts of the theory itself.

First a few words concerning method. If we desire to analyze a dream, we proceed exactly as in the psychological investigation of psychoneurotic symptoms. Behind each imperative thought, no matter how illogical it may appear, are hidden coherent but unconscious thoughts, and to make these evident is the problem of psychoanalysis. Freud has proved that the images and experiences of which the dream consists, are for the most part only disguises, symbolic allusions to suppressed trains of thought. Behind the *conscious dream-content is hidden a latent dream-material, which, on its part, was aroused by coherent, logical dream-thoughts.* The interpretation of the dream is nothing else than the translation of the dream from its hieroglyphic-symbolic speech into conceptual speech; the leading back of the obvious dream-content through the clues of association given by the hidden dream-material, to the logical dream-thoughts. The means by which this is done is the socalled free association. We have the dream related to us, divide the given material into several parts or sections, and require the dreamer to tell all that occurs to him when he directs his attention, not to the whole of the dream, but to a definite part of it, to a particular event or word-image occurring in it. This association must, however, be wholly free, consequently the single thing forbidden is the dominance of critical choice among the irruptive ideas. Any halfway intelligent man can be brought to tell out all the thoughts associated with the fragments of the dream, whether clever or stupid, coherent or senseless, pleasant or unpleasant, suppressing the shame perhaps bound up with them. In this way also are worked over the other fragments of the dream and so we assemble the latent dream material, that is to say, all the thoughts and memories of which the conscious dream picture is to be considered the condensation-product (*Verdichtungsprodukt*). It is an error to believe that the activity of association when left free is devoid of any regulation by law. As soon as in the analysis we disregard the conscious terminal idea (*Zielvorstellung*) of our thinking, the directive forces of the unconscious psychic activities prevail in the choice of associations, that is to say, just the same mental forces which functioned in the creation of the dream. We have been for a long time familiar with the thought that there is no chance in the physical world, no event without sufficient cause; on the ground of psychoanalytic experience we must suppose just as strong a determination of every mental activity, however arbitrary it may seem. It is therefore an unjustified fear that the activity of association when freed from all restraints in such analysis, will give results which have no value. The subject of the analysis, who at first reproduces his apparently senseless ideas with scornful scepticism, soon discovers, to his own surprise, that the train of associations, uninfluenced by conscious aids, leads to the awakening ot thoughts and memories which were long since forgotten, or repressed on account of the pain they caused. But through the emergence of these the fragment taken from the dream is made intelligible or capable of interpretation. If we repeat this process with all the parts of the dream, we see that the trains of thought which radiate out from the different fragments converge in a very essential train of thought, which was stimulated the day before the night of the dream the dream thoughts themselves. Once these are recognized, not only the single fragment, but also the dream as a whole seems coherent and intelligible. If, finally, we compare the point of departure of the dream, the dream thoughts, with the content of the naively related dream, we see that *the dream is nothing else than the concealed fulfillment of a repressed wish.*

This sentence contains the most essential results of Freud's investigation of dreams. The idea that the dream fulfills wishes, which in the rude world of facts must be unfulfilled, seems to share in the language of abandoned popular science. "Dreams" are used metaphorically in most languages for "wishes" and the Hungarian proverb says just this, that "swine dream of acorns, the goose of maize" which is only to be regarded as an allusion to the similar direction of human dreams.

Some of the dreams of adults and most of the dreams of children are purely wish-fulfillment dreams. The child dreams of pleasureable experiences denied him by day, of the toys which he envied his little comrades, of victorious struggles with those of his own age, of his good mother, or his friendly father. Very often in his dream he seems "big," endowed with all the freedom and power of his parents, which he wishes for so ardently by day. Wish dreams like these also occur to adults. The difficult test (about which we are so anxious) seems in dreams splendidly passed, dear relatives awaken from their graves and assure us that they are not dead, we appear to ourselves rich, powerful, endowed with great oratorical gifts, the most beautiful of women solicit our favor, and so on. For the most part we attain in dreams just that which we painfully miss on waking.

The same tendency to wish-fulfillment rules not only nocturnal, but day dreams as well, the fancies in which we can catch ourselves at unoccupied moments or during monotonous activity. Freud has observed that women's fancies deal for the most part with things which immediately or mediately belong to the sex life (of being loved, proposals, beautiful clothes), those of men predominantly with power and esteem, but also with sexual satisfaction.

Fancies concerning the means of escape from a real or imagined danger and the annihilation of real or imagined enemies are also very common. These simple wish-fulfillment dreams and fancies have an obvious meaning, and need no particular labor for their interpretation.

But that which is new, surprising and incredible to many in Freud's explanation of dreams is the assertion that all dreams, even those which seem indifferent or even unpleasant, can be reduced to this basal form, and that it can be shown by analysis that they fulfill wishes in a disguised way. In order to understand this, we must first make ourselves familiar with the mechanism of psychic activity in dreams.

The associative analysis of a dream is only the reversal of the *synthetic* work which the psyche executes at night while it transforms the unwelcome thought and the unpleasant sensation which disturb sleep into wish-fulfilling dream-images. By a critical consideration one is convinced that this work never ceases during sleep, even when after waking we cannot recall that we dreamed at all. The traditional idea that dreams disturb rest during sleep must be abandoned on the ground of these newly won results ; on the contrary, since they do not allow the unpleasant, painful or burdensome thought which would disturb sleep to become conscious with its true content, but in a changed form as the fulfillment of a wish, we are forced to recognize dreams as the preservers of sleep. -

The psychic factor which watches over rest during sleep, often with the assistance of the dream disguise already mentioned, is the censor. This is the gate-keeper at the threshold of consciousness, which we see zealously at work during waking life also, especially in psychoneuroses, and which for our problem is to be considered as either repressing all thought groupings which are distasteful in aesthetic or ethical ways, or disguising them in the form of apparently harmless symbols, symptomatic acts or symptomatic thoughts.

The function of the censorship is to secure the repose of consciousness and to keep at a distance all psychic creations which would cause pain or disturb rest. And like the censor of political absolutism, who sometimes works at night, the psychic censorship is kept in activity during sleep, though its red penciling is not so strongly in evidence as in waking life. Probably the censor is led to relax its activity by the idea that the motor reactions are paralyzed during sleep, and so thoughts cannot be expressed in deeds. So the fact may be explained that for the most part those images and situations emerge as wish fulfillments in dreams which we refuse by day to recognize as wishes.

We all shelter in our unconscious ego many wishes repressed since childhood, which take the opportunity of exercising their psychic intensity as soon as they perceive the letting down of the censorship at night.

It is not chance that among the wishes revealed in dreams, the strongly repressed sexual excitations, and in particular those of the most contemptible kind play the greatest r6le. It is a very great error to believe that psychoanalysis intention- ally places sexual activity in the foreground. It cannot be denied that whenever one seeks to investigate thoroughly the basal facts of mental life, he always strikes against the sexual elements. If, accordingly, we find psychoanalysis objectionable for this reason, we are really degrading the description of the unconscious facts of human mentality by our action in regarding them as obscene. The censorship of affairs of sex is, as already said, much milder in dream life than during waking hours, so that in dreams we experience and crave sexual experiences without bounds, even representing in our dreams experiences and acts reminding one of the so-called perversions. I avail myself as an example of the dream of a patient who was extraordinarily modest in waking life. He saw himself enveloped in an antique peplum, fastened in front with a safety-pin; suddenly the pin fell out, the white garment opened in front, and his nakedness was admired by a great crowd of men. Another, equally modest patient, told me this, which is an exhibition dream with somewhat altered circumstances: She was enveloped from top to toe in a white garment and bound to a pillar; around her stood foreign men, Turks or Arabs, who were haggling over her. The scene reminds one very strongly, apart from her enveloping garment, of an Oriental slave market; and, indeed, analysis brought out that this lady, now so modest, when a young girl had read the tales of the "Thousand and One Nights," and had seen herself in fancy in many of the situations of the highly colored love scenes of the Orient. At that time she imagined that slaves were exposed for sale not clothed, but naked. At present she repudiates the idea of nudity so strongly even in dreams that the suppressed wishes which bear upon this theme can only come into being *when changed to their opposite*. A third dreamer only allowed herself so much freedom in this respect as to move about in the midst of the other forms of her dream incompletely clad, in her stockings or with bare feet; and here analysis showed that as a child for a long time she enjoyed greatly removing her clothes and going without them, so that she was nicknamed "the naked Pancri" (her name was Anna, in Hungarian Fauna). Such exhibition dreams are so frequent that Freud was able to put them in the class of his "typical dreams," which recur with most people from time to time and have the same origin. They are based on the fact that there is living on in all of us an undying longing for the return of the paradisical conditions of childhood; this is the " golden age," that poets and Utoplans project from the past into the future. It is a very common means of dream disguise to circumvent the censorship by presenting the wish not as such, but only in the form of an allusion in the dream. It would not be possible to understand, for example, why one of my patients dreamed so often of sexual scenes with a man by the name of Frater, who was quite indifferent to her, if we had not learned that in her youth her brother (*frater*) was her ideal and that in childhood the affection of the pair had often taken on a purely erotic form and manifested itself by relations that she now repressed as incestuous. This repression of forbidden things often enters into the dream, especially with persons who in consequence of incomplete satisfaction of the libido are inclined to the development of anxiety (Freud's anxiety-neurotics). Nocturnal anxiety can become so great that the dreamer awakens with feelings of pain (*pavor nocturnus*). Anxiety which has a physiological basis, gives in such cases an opportunity for the deeply repressed childishperverse excitations to involve themselves in the dream, in the form of frightful, cruel, horrible scenes, which seem frightful to us, but in a certain depth of the unconscious satisfy wishes which in the "prehistoric" ages of our own mental development were actually recognized as desires.

The great part played in such dreams by cruelties inflicted or suffered must find its explanation in the sadistic idea which children have of the sex-relationship, as Freud has so beautifully shown in his "infantile sexual theories." All the cruel acts of such dreams appear in analysis as sexual events transformed into deeds of violence. Sexually unsatisfied women, for example, very commonly dream of thieves breaking in, of attacks by robbers or wild beasts; but not one of the concealed, well-hidden incidents of the dream betrays that the outrages to which the dreamer is subjected really symbolize sexual acts. An hysterical of my observation once dreamed that she was run down by a bull before which she held a red garment. There was involved in this dream not only the present wish to possess such a dress, but also an unavowed sexual wish, the same which also caused the sickness. The thought of the frightfully enraged bull, which is a widespread symbol of manly strength, came to her especially through the circumstance that a man with a so-called "bull neck" had played a certain rôle in the development of her sexual life.

Childish memories make continual and always significant contributions to the creation of the dream. Freud has also established the fact that the earliest age of childhood is not only not free from sexual excitations, but that rather infantile sexuality, not yet restrained by education, is expressly of a perverse character. In infantile sexuality the oral and analurethral erogeneous zones, the partial impulses

(*Partialtriebe*) of sexual curiosity and of exhibitionism, as well as sadistic and mashochistic impulses rule. When we consider these facts we come to the conclusion that Freud is in the right when he says that dreams express such impulses as wish-fulfillments, as the fulfillment of wishes from that part of our childhood which seems long since outgrown.

There are, however, dreams of very unpleasant content, which peculiarly enough disturb our rest hardly at all, so that when we awaken we reproach ourselves for experiencing such terrible events with so little sympathy or feeling. This sort of dream was observed, for example, by one of Freud's patients, who in a dream was present at the funeral of a beloved nephew. An apparently unessential detail of the dream, a concert ticket, led to the explanation of such an occurrence. The lady intended to attend a concert on the next night, where she expected to see again the man whom she formerly loved and had not yet forgotten, whom she had met for the last time a long while before, at the funeral of another nephew. So the dream, in order to hasten the meeting, sacrificed the other nephew. But the censorship, seemingly knowing that by the dream a harmless wish, and not that of death, was to be fulfilled, let the funeral "pass," without attaching to it any obvious emotional excitation. This analysis may serve as an example for all those dreams which apparently contradict Freud's wish theory, and which have to do with very unwelcome things or even with the non-fulfillment of wishes. If we seek out the latent dream thoughts concealed behind these painfully toned dreams, it becomes clear to us that, as Freud himself expresses it *the non-fulfillment of a wish in a dream always means the fulfillment of some other wish.*

When we consider the materials of the dream gained by free association from the conscious dream elements, it becomes clear that they flow pretty generally from two opposed sources; from childhood memories on the one hand, and from unobserved experiences of the "dream day," often quite indifferent, which were not reacted to. Indeed, according to Freud's expression, every well- articulated dream stands as it were on two legs, and is shown by analysis to be *over-determined* (*Ucberdeierminierf*), that is, to be the fulfillment of both a present and a long suppressed wish.

As an example I may relate the dream of a patient suffering from a nervous difficulty in urination. "A polished floor, wet, as though a pool lay there. Two chairs leaning against the wall. As I look around, I note that the front legs of both chairs are missing, as when one wants to play a joke on someone and has him sit down on a broken chair, and he falls. One of my friends was also there with her affianced."

Free association on the theme of the polished floor gave the fact that on the day before her brother in a rage had thrown a pitcher to the floor, which, with the water spilled over it, looked like the floor in the dream. She also remembered a similar floor from her childhood. On this occasion her brother, who was then very young, had made her laugh so hard that micturition ensued. This part of the dream, which also proved significant for the symptom-creation of the neurosis, accordingly fulfilled infantile erotic wishes which could now in consequence of strong censorship be presented only in allusions. The two broken chairs leaning against the wall were shown by analysis to be a scenic presentation of the proverb "To fall to the ground between two stools" (that is, to be deceived from two directions). The patient had already had two suitors, but the family constellation already mentioned (the unconscious love for her brother) prevented the marriage on both occasions. And although her unconscious ego, according to her repeated testimony, had long been reconciled to the thought of spinsterhood, she still seems in the depth of her soul to have regarded with some envy the recent betrothal of one of her friends. The affianced couple had in fact been calling on her the day before.

According to Freud's theory we can picture to ourselves the origin of this dream in the following way: The dream-work succeeded in uniting two experiences of the day before, the breaking of the pitcher and the visit of the betrothed pair, with that train of thought, always emotively toned, which, though already suppressed in childhood, was always in condition to lend its affective energy to any present mental image which could be brought into even a superficial connection with it. Freud compares the dream to the promotion of a business undertaking, in which the unconscious, suppressed complex furnishes the capital, that is, the affective energy, while the wishes play the role of promoters.

Another source of dreams is in those sensory and sensible nerve-stimulations to which the organism is subject during sleep. These may be: dermal stimuli, the pressure of mattress and covering, cooling of the skin; acoustic or optical stimuli to which the sleeper is subjected; organic sensations: hunger, thirst, an overloaded stomach; a stimulated condition of the sex parts, and so on. Most psychologists and physiologists are inclined to attribute too great significance to stimuli of this sort; they think that they have given a satisfactory explanation of all dreams when they say that the dream is nothing but the sum of such psychophysic reactions, set free by nerve stimuli of this character. On the other hand, Freud rightly says that the dream does not admit these bodily stimuli as such to consciousness, but disguises and alters them in particular ways; the motive and means of this disguise are given not through the outer stimuli, but from mental sources of energy. The nerve stimuli during sleep offer then, as it were, only the opportunity for the unfolding of certain immanent tendencies of the psychic life. Analysis shows that dreams caused by nerve stimulation are also open or concealed wish-fulfillments: the thirsty man drinks great amounts of water in his dreams, the hungry man satisfies himself; the sick man who is disturbed by the ice-packing on his head throws it away, for he thinks of himself in his dream as already well; the painful throbbing of a boil on the perinaeum leads to the dream idea of riding. So it is made possible that the hunger, the thirst, the pressure on the head, the painful inflammation, do not waken the sleeper, but are transmitted into wish-fulfillments by the psychic forces.

The anxiety-dream known as "*Alpdruck*" brought on by an overloaded stomach, respiratory disturbances or disturbances of the circulation, or by intoxication, permits of explanation in the same way; the unpleasant bodily sensations offer an opportunity for deeply repressed wishes to fulfill themselves, wishes which the censorship of culture will not allow to pass and which can break into consciousness only in connection with feelings of anxiety and disgust.

In the process of analysis, as already said, we retrace, only in the reverse direction, the same way which the sleeping soul has travelled in the creation of the dream. And when we compare the manifest dream, often very short, with the rich material which is brought to light during the process of analysis, and when we consider that in spite of this quantitative difference all the elements of the latent dream-content are contained in some way in the portion which is manifest to us, we must agree that Freud is right when he considers this dream-condensation as the most toilsome part of the creation of the dream. I will attempt to show this by an example. A patient suffering from psychosexual impotence brought to me on one occasion a dream made up of two fragments. In the first fragment the only occurrence was that instead of a Hungarian paper, "Pesti Holap," which regularly came to him, he received the Vienna "Neue Freie Presse," to which as a matter of fact one of his colleagues subscribed. The second fragment of the dream dealt with a brunette, whom he wanted to marry at any price. It turned out that he acquired in his dream not the foreign paper, but in the hidden sense of the dream, a foreign woman, to whom in fact a colleague had "subscribed." This woman had long excited his interest, for it seemed to him that just this person could bring to functioning his sexuality which was struggling with strong inhibitions. The thought associations which came from this idea made it clear that he had been deceived in his hopes of another woman, with whom, with the same object in view, he had entered into a lasting relation. This woman, since she was a Hungarian, he had concealed in the dream behind the name of the paper "Pesti Holap." Of late he had occupied himself in seeking *free* sexual associations, which led to no obligations, instead of such more stable relations. When we know the great freedom with which the dream avails itself of symbols, we are not surprised to learn that my patient also applied the word "Press" in a sexual sense. The second part of the dream shows, as though it wished to confirm our interpretation, that the patient had often been obliged to think, not without anxiety, that relations which lasted too long, like that between himself and his friend, could easily lead to a mesalliance. One who does not know that, as Freud has shown in his monograph, the psychic motive and means of presentation of wit are almost exactly the same as those which come out in dreams, might consider us guilty of cheap wit in saying that the dream succeeds in condensing in the words "Neue Freie Presse" all the patient's thoughts and wishes which concerned themselves with the pleasures of which his sickness had robbed him, and the means of benefit which he had in mind, namely, the stimulus of the new and the greater freedom for which he was striving.

(Novelty and journal are expressed in Hungarian by the same word "zg'sag.")

Very characteristic products of the dream-condensation are the composite images (Misc/zbildungm) of persons, objects and words. These "monstrosities of the dream world" have contributed largely to the fact that dreams up to our day have been regarded as productions of the mind which were without value and without sense. But psychoanalysis convinces us that when the dream links together or fuses two features or concepts, it furnishes a less successful product of the same work of condensation to which the less obvious parts of the dream owe their disguise. One of the rules of the art of dream interpretation states that in cases of such composite images the dream material of the single constituents must first be sought, and then only can it be determined on what basis ofa common element or similarity

74

the welding together has taken place. An example of this, which is theoretically valuable, I owe to one of my patients. The Composite picture which occurred in one of her dreams, was made up of the person of a physician and of a horse, which in addition was attired in night clothing. Associations led from the horse into the childhood of the patient. She suffered as a girl for a long time from a pronounced phobia of horses; she avoided them particularly on account of their obvious and open satisfaction of their bodily needs. In addition it occured to her that as a child she had often been taken by her nurse to the military quarters, where she had had the opportunity to observe all these things with a curiosity which was at that time still unrestrained. The night clothing reminded her of her father, whom she had had the opportunity, to see, while she still slept in the room of her parents, not only in such costume, but in the act of satisfying his bodily needs. (This is a frequently repeated case; parents for the most part put no restraint on themselves before three and four-year old children, whose understanding and faculty of observation they materially underestimate.) The third constituent of the composite picture, the physician, awakened in me the suspicion, which proved to be well grounded, that the patient had unconsciously transferred her sexual curiosity from her father to the physician who was treating her.

Many times the constituent parts of a composite person have an unequal share in its creation; perhaps only a characteristic movement of one person is grafted on to the second person. I saw myself once in a dream rub my forehead with my hand just as my honored master, Professor Freud, does, when he is meditating over a hard question. It does not require much art of interpretation to guess that this mixing of teacher and pupil, especially in meditation, can only be blamed to envy and ambition, when at night the intellectual censorship was relaxed. In my waking life I have to laugh at the boldness of this identification, which strongly reminds one of the sentence, "How he clears his throat and how he spits, that have you bravely learned from him." As an example of a composite word, I may say that in a dream a German speaking patient thought of a certain Metzler or Wetzler. Persons with such names are, however, unknown to the patient. He was, however, very much occupied on the day before with the approaching marriage of a friend, by the name of Messer, who liked to joke (*hetzen*)–South-German for *necken*–with the patient. The associations from Messer showed that he as a small child had been greatly in fear of his grandfather, who, while whetting (*wetzen*) his pocket-knife (*Taschenmesser*) had jokingly threatened him with castration, a threat which was not without influence on the development of his sexuality. The name "Metzler-Wetzler" are accordingly nothing but condensations of the words *messer*, *hetzen* and *wetzen*.

Dream condensation stands in close relation with the work of displacement and transvaluation (*Verschiebungsarbeit*) of the dream. This consists essentially in the fact that the psychic intensity of the dream thoughts is shunted over from the essentials to the accessories, so that the thought-complex which is at the focus of interest is represented in the conscious dream content either not at all or by a weak allusion, while the maximum of interest in the dream is turned to the more insignificant constituents of the dream thoughts. The work of condensation and displacement go hand in hand. The dream makes harmless an important thought, which would disturb the rest of the sleeper, or be censured on ethical grounds. It as it were goes beyond such a thought, by attaching to its more unessential parts memory images until the condensed psychic intensity of these latter is able to distract the attention from the particularly interesting thought. As an example of the displaced centre of the conscious dream in comparison with the centre of the dream thoughts I may mention the already cited dream of the aunt concerning the death of her beloved, nephew. The actually non-essential funeral took up the largest place in the dream, the personality which was very significant for the dream thoughts was on the contrary present in the dream only through a distant allusion.

I was once called upon to analyze the very short dream of a woman; she had wrung the neck of a little barking, white dog. She was very much amazed that she, who ' 'could not hurt a fly" could dream such a cruel dream; she did not remember having had one like it before. She admitted that she was very fond of cooking and that many times she had with her own hands killed chickens and doves. Then it occurred to her that she had wrung the neck of the little dog in her dream in exactly the same way that she was accustomed to do with the doves in order to cause the birds less pain. The thoughts and associations which followed had to do with pictures and stories of executions, and especially with the thought that the executioner, when he has fastened the cord about the neck of the criminal, arranges it so as to give the neck a twist, to hasten death. Asked against whom she felt strong enmity at the present time, she named a sister-in-law, and related at length her bad qualities and the malicious deeds, with which she had disturbed the family harmony, before so beautiful, after insinuating herself like a *tame dove* into the favor of her later husband. Not long before there had taken place between her and the patient a very violent scene, which ended by the patient showing the other woman the door with the words: "Get out; I cannot endure a biting dog in my house." Now it was clear whom the little white dog represented, and whose neck she wrung in her dream. The sister-in-law is also a small person, with an extraordinarily white complexion. This little analysis enables us to observe the dream in its displacing and so disguising activity.

Without doubt the dream has used the comparison with the biting dog, instead of the real object of the execution-fancy (the sister-in-law), smuggling in a little white dog, just as the angel in the Biblical story gave Abraham a ram to slaughter at the last instant, when he was preparing to sacrifice his son. In order to accomplish this, the dream had to heap up memory images of the killing of animals until by means of their condensed psychic energy the image of the hated person paled, and the scene of the obvious dream was shifted to the animal kingdom. Memory images of human executions serves as a connecting link for this displacement.

This example gives me the opportunity to repeat that, with few exceptions, the conscious dream-content is not the true reproduction of our dream thoughts, but only a displaced wrongly accented caricature, whose original can only be reconstructed by the help of psychoanalysis.

It is a noteworthy phenomenon of dream work that the material of abstract thought, the concept, is capable of presentation in the dream only little or not at all, that rather the dream as it were dramatizes thoughts only in optic or acoustic sense images, changes them to scenes enacted on a stage, and in this way brings them to presentation. Freud characterizes very strikingly the difficulty which this necessity of working only with concrete material imposes upon the dream, when he says that the dream itself has to turn the thoughts of a political editorial into illustrations.

Dreams are fond of using ambiguous words and interpretations of all sorts of expressions in concrete or metaphorical senses in order to make abstract concepts and thoughts capable of presentation and so of inclusion in the dream.

The memory of every halfway educated man contains a large number of proverbs, quotations, modes of expression, parables, fragments of verse and so forth. The content of these offers an ever present, very suitable material which can be applied to the scenic presentation of a thought or to an allusion to it. I will attempt to explain this by a series of examples. One of my patients related to me the following dream; "I go into a great park, walking on a long path. I cannot see the end of the path or of the garden hedge, but I think I will go on until I arrive at the end." The park and hedge of the dream resembled the garden of one of her aunts, with whom she had passed many happy holidays of her youth. She remembers in connection with this aunt that they customarily shared the same chamber, but when her uncle was at home the guest was "put out" into a neighboring room. The girl at that time only had a very fragmentary conception of the affairs of sex, and tried often by peeping through cracks in the door and through the keyhole, to find out what was going on within.

The wish to get to the end of the hedge symbolized in this dream the wish to get to the bottom of what was going on between the married pair. This wish was moreover determined by an experience of the day before.

Another patient dreamed of the corridor of the girls' boarding school in which she was educated. She saw her own closet there, and desired to open it, but could not find the key, so that she was forced to break the door. But as she violently opened the door, it became evident that there was nothing within. The whole dream proved to be a symbolic masturbation-phantasy, a memory from the time of puberty; the female genitals were, as so often happens, presented as a closet. But the supplement to the dream, "there is nothing within" (*es ist nichts darin*) means in the Hungarian language the same as the German expression "it is no matter" (*es ist nichts daran*), and is a sort of exculpation or self-consolation of this sufferer from a bad conscience.

Another girl, whose neurosis was brought on by the death of her brother, who, according to her view, married too early and was not happy in his marriage, dreamed continually of the dead man. Once she saw him lying in his grave, but the head was turned to one side in a peculiar manner, or the skull had grown to a bough; another time she saw him in his childhood dress on an elevation from which he had to jump down. All this symbolism was a complaint against the wife and the fatherin-law of the dead man, who turned the boy's head, when he was almost a child, and in the end made him "jump down" (which is a pure Hungarian idiom), and with all that did not consider him as their equal, for they once called him, referring to his modest origin, "one fallen from a bough" (again a Hungarian idiom).

Very often falling from a great height pictures in a concrete way the threat of ethical or material fall; with girls sitting may mean spinsterhood (*Sitzenbleiben*); with men a great basket may mean the fear of an unsuccessful wooing. It occurs still more commonly that the human body is symbolized by a house, whose windows and doors symbolize the natural openings of the body. My patient who suffered from sexual impotence made use of a trivial Hungarian expression for coitus, namely the word "to shoot," and dreamed very often of shooting, missing fire, the rusting of his firearms, and so forth.

It would be an enticing problem to assemble the fragments of dreams which can be explained symbolically and to write a modern dreambook, in which the explanation could be found for the separate parts of dreams. But this is not possible, for although much typical material recurs in dreams and in most cases can be rightly explained without analysis, symbols may have different meanings with different individuals, and even with the same individual at different times. Accordingly, if we wish to know in any particular case all the determinants of the single dream fragments there is nothing left for us but painful analysis, for which the investigating power and the wit of the interpreter of the dream alone will not suffice, but the industrious co-operation of the dreamer is indispensable.

Still greater difficulties than are created by the presentation of abstract thoughts are met when the dream attempts to present in a concrete way the thought relations of the single dream- thoughts. It is Freud's valuable service to have succeeded in making it possible to discover the whole of the hidden formal peculiarities of the articulation of the dream, with which the dream attempts to present logical relations. Logical relations between two dream elements with respect to the dreamthoughts which are hidden behind them, are presented in the simplest case by temporal, spatial proximity, or by a fusion of the features of the dream.

The dream lacks a means of presentation of causal connection, of the either-or relation of conditions, and so forth, so that all these relations are brought to presentation in a very insufficient way by means of a temporal sequence of the dream elements. From this fact arise many embarrassments for the interpreter of dreams, and often only the communications of the dreamer can extricate him. But much may be guessed. For example, if a dream picture changes to another, we can divine behind this, cause and effect; but this connection the dream often presents by two completely separated dreams, one of which signifies the cause, the other the effect. Even in the presentation of a simple negative the dream can succeed only with great difficulty, so that as we know from Freud we can never tell in advance whether the dream thought is to be interpreted in a positive or a negative way. Considering the complexities of our mental organism it is only too easily seen that affirmation and negation of the same thoughts and feelingcomplexes is to be met with in the dream thoughts side by side, or, rather in succession. It may be taken as a sign of displeasure and scorn when anything in a dream is presented in a reversed form, or when the truth is presented very openly and in a striking way. The feeling of inhibition, which is so common, signifies a conflict of the will, the struggle of opposing motives.

Now in spite of the lack of all logical relations in the change of the dream thoughts into the manifest dream, the latter often seems to be possessed of sense and to be correlated. When this is the case, it may result from one of two causes. We may be concerned on the one hand with a dreamphantasy, that is, with the reproduction of fancies which have grown up in the waking life, articles read in books or journals, fragments of romances or bits of conversation spoken or heard by the person himself. A deeper and more general explanation for the apparently logical articulation of many dreams is, however, the fact that the rationalizing tendency of mental activity, which seeks to arrange senseless material into logical' trains of thought, does not rest at night. This last activity of the dream Freud calls the *secondary working-over* (*sekundäre Bearbeitung*) . It is due to this that the originally fragmentary parts of the dream are rounded out to a whole by supplementarily inserted connecting words and other little connections.

Because the dream has fundamentally condensed, displaced, disguised, scenically presented a dream thought, robbed it of its logical connections and worked it over in a secondary way, the work of interpretation is often very difficult. We are confronted by the conscious dream-content as by a hieroglyph or by a rebus which is very difficult of solution, and as a result the explanation of many dreams needs, besides the rules of Freud's interpretation, an especial capacity and inclination to occupy oneself with questions of the mental life.

Not less a riddle than the dream itself is its rapid fading out after awakening. When we awake the dream images so toilsomely built up at night collapse like a house of cards. During sleep the mind is like an air-tight room, into which neither light nor sound can penetrate from without, but within its own walls the slightest sound, even the buzzing of a fly, can be heard. But awakening is like opening the door to the air of the bright morning; through the doors of our senses press in the bustle and the impulses of everyday life, and the daily cares, lately soothed to sleep by wish-fancies, again take up their reign. The censor, too, awakes from its slumber, and its first act is to declare the dream to be " foolishness," to explain it as senseless, to put it as it were under guardianship. It is not always satisfied with this measure, it reacts much more strongly against the revolutionary dreams (and there is not a single dream which cannot be shown by analysis to offend against some ethical or legal canon). The stronger method consists in the confiscation, the full suppression of the dream image. Mental confiscation is usually called "forgetting." One relates with wonder how clearly he dreamed, and yet when he woke all was confused and in a few minutes he had forgotten it all. At other times one can only say that the dream was beautiful, good, bad, confused, stimulating, or stupid. Even in making this judgment many times a remnant of the dream content will show itself, whose analysis can lead to a later recovery of larger fragments of the dream. Behind such additional fragments of the dream brought to light in this way one often finds the kernel of the dream-thoughts.

It is an important consequence of Freud's theory of dreams, that one is always dreaming, so long as he sleeps. That one remembers nothing of this is no decisive objection against this consideration. My patients, for example, who at the beginning of the analysis declared that they had usually no dreams, gradually accustomed themselves by continual weakening of the inner psychic resistance against the censorship to remember all their dreams. But if in the course of the analysis one strikes a very resistant, pain-toned complex, dreams apparently cease naturally they are only forgotten, repressed, because of their unpleasant content.

The obvious objection, that these dream observations and analyses have been carried on for the most part on neurotic and so abnormal persons, and that conclusions should not be drawn as to the dreams of healthy people, does not need to be refuted by the reply that mental health and psychoneuroses only differ in a quantitative way; it can also be answered that the analyses of people mentally normal fully agree with the interpretation of dreams of neurotics. The communication of the analysis of one's own dreams, however, meets with almost insurmountable difficulties. Freud has not shrunk from this sacrifice the exposure of intimate personal matters in his "*Traumdeutung*," even though regard for others make unavoidable gaps here and there in his analyses. Similar considerations made it necessary for me to explain the art of the interpretation of dreams not from my own dreams, but from those of my patients. For the rest, the practise of selfanalysis is indispensable for anyone who desires to penetrate into the unconscious processes of dream-life.

The neurotic persons whose dreams I have brought forward here and there as examples also pave the way for me to say a few words about the pathological and therapeutic significance of dreams and their interpretation. We saw how greatly the analysis of a neurotic may be accelerated by a successful dream analysis. The dream censorship, which is only half awake, often allows to penetrate to the dream consciousness thought-complexes, which in waking life could not be brought to consciousness by free association. There also lead out from the dream elements immediate and shorter ways to the repressed pathogenic material, that is, to the source of the neurotic symptoms. The becoming conscious of such complexes can be regarded as a step toward the cure.

Then, too, the diagnostic significance of dreams must not escape us, and in a time which is not too distant there ought to arise besides the physiological, also a pathological dream psychology, which should treat systematically of the peculiarities of dreams with hystericals, those suffering from imperative neuroses, paranoiacs, dementia prsecox patients, sufferers from neurasthenia, from the anxiety-neurosis, alcoholism, epilepsy, paralysis, sub-normals, etc. Many pathognostic peculiarities of dreams in these diseased conditions are already recognizable today.

All these more practical and special questions were raised to importance by the unexpected theoretical consequences of this investigation of dreams. Freud has succeeded in surprising a process on the boundary line between the physiological and pathological departments of mental life, in taking it in the midst of its work, inflagranti, as it were. In this way he has brought us nearer to an understanding of the mechanism of the manifestations of neuroses and insanity in waking life. And though it was the study of psychoneuroses which led Freud to his investigation of dreams, the dream theory pays back with interest all that it owes to pathology.

The case could indeed not be other than it is. Waking, dreams, neuroses and psychoses are only variations of the same psychic material with different modes of functioning, and progressive insight into one of these processes must necessarily deepen and widen our knowledge of the others.

Those who expect from the new dream theory any sort of prophetic insight into the future will turn back disillusioned. But those who value highly the solution of psychological problems held until now as insoluble, the widening of the psychological point of view apart from any immediate practical consequences, and who are not held back from advance by hide-bound prejudices, such will perhaps supplement the communication given here by a thorough and earnest study of Freud's *"Traumdeutung."*

www.ingramcontent.com/pod-product-compliance
Lightning Source LLC
Chambersburg PA
CBHW062038280526
45788CB00003B/1035